Miles & Coltrane: Blue(.)

Concrete Generation

Copyright © 2012 Author Name

All rights reserved.

The amateur and professional live stage performance rights to Miles & Coltrane: Blue (.) are controlled exclusively by Blue Period The Play, LLC and all licensing arrangements and performances licenses must be obtained by contacting Concrete Generation. All other rights of every kind and nature, including but not limited to television, video or audio taping, in whole or in part, or any other form of mechanical or electronic reproduction, such as information storage and retrieval systems and photocopying, are reserved by the author(s) and are not included in this authorization. Reproduction of any kind, including for personal use, is also strictly prohibited.

ISBN: 0615846254
ISBN-13:9780615846255

This Book Is Dedicated To Each And Every Artist,
Their Journey As A Creative Being And The Dreams In Which They Believe

CONTENTS

1	Icons of Artistry	Pg. 10
2	The Aura Still Prevails	Pg. 17
3	Sunday Prayer Service	Pg. 28
4	Music. Music. Music.	Pg. 43
5	Get In Your Veins	Pg. 50
6	Addiction	Pg. 55
7	A Love Supreme	Pg. 67
8	Dear Miles	Pg. 75
9	God Said It Was Good	Pg. 77
10	Pretty Faced Strumpets	Pg. 81
11	Uppity Nigga	Pg. 89
12	This Is How I Pray	Pg. 93
13	And It Came To Past	Pg. 101

This work is a true jazz piece; meaning structure is important, but never be afraid to vamp and improv. This is especially true of the musicians, whether it is a trio or a full orchestra. The band should think in terms of score and concert mode, fluctuating between the two seamlessly. There are two actors who take on the persona of Miles & Coltrane; additionally, there are two dancers who respectively take on their personas. The Griot and The Storyteller are poets at heart and narrate the journey in beat/slam/concrete performance poetry fashion. They often interact with Miles & Coltrane actors and get us from one transition to the next. The ensemble is a suite movement between each artist, playing off of one another; Hence this piece is not just about jazz, but performed as a work of jazz. And last but definitely not least; Above all else, keep it progressive. And there will be no two shows that are alike.

The Characters-

Miles (the human)/(the here and now)
Coltrane (the being)/(always trying to elevate)
The Storyteller
The Griot
Heroin
The Voice(.)
The Voice of Alice Coltrane
The Voice of the Pretty Face Strumpets

The Sessions- band
Major- Trumpet   Minor- Saxophone
Theory- Bass   Improv- Piano
Riff- Drums

The Atmosphere-

The costumes: we be fly as hell...
act accordingly

The set: can be minimalistic or grandiose...
depends on what kind of ends you got

The lighting: simple yet complex, traditional yet
modern...transition into style

The music: classic, contemporary, original

Miles & Coltrane: Blue (.)

The man who wanted to be god on earth
& the man who was a falling saint

Concrete Generation

Miles & Coltrane: Blue (.)

Miles & Coltrane: Blue (.)

Miles & Coltrane: Blue (.)

The year was 1953,
and the psyche of America is in flux.

Hung over from the Korean war
The youth of the nation are restless.

Not the usual restlessness of
adolescence teenage angst,
but the restlessness of the soul.

Seeking to shed the false comfort of conformity,
from the propaganda of the cold war,
to the promotion of the American way;
seeking for what they know in their hearts is truth.

It was the height of the Beat-
as Ginsberg, Burroughs, Kerouac,
Baraka, Snyder, Cassidy
and other luminaries introduced
the idea of the free
         thinker.

Abstract expression
      as a means
of social critique,
      and the notion
of the individual
      embracing personal
freedom

while resisting institutional values.

Marlon Brando and James dean,
the angry young man
            and the rebel without a cause,
were the brightest stars
in the Hollywood galaxy.

With the rise of Civil Rights
with the Montgomery Alabama
bus boycotts-

there was a raising
of consciousness for both blacks
and whites and

everybody
was
Angry,
   Cool,
      High,
         and hip-
Yet sophisticated
   and ultra clean.

The New Radicals.

And the soundtrack to this social revolution was Jazz.
And on the forefront of jazz music
was Miles Davis & John Coltrane.

Icons of Artistry-
We call this new age expression
Blue (.)
                    Let the sessions begin...

Ladies and Gentleman,
 tonight in this session,
introducing the past to progression,

We present to you

      on trumpet

A man who wanted to be

      god on earth

none other than the infamous

Miles Davis.

Also introducing

the future

to sound

We present on tenor

        and soprano saxophone

The man who was

        a

            falling

                angel   None other than

   the saint   John William
Coltrane.

Miles & Coltrane: Blue (.)

After the cool shit

Before the crazy

        Lets make music

High as hell shit

Miles set out accomplished

        (shhitt)

Set out again just to

Accomplish

        (new always)

On the forefront

        (Something new always)

Blow boy blow

        (Grab a trumpet.

                Afterwards

  grab some

young pretty coke

    bottle

waste

spike vain in veins

with vain waste

sexy slim cutter

with a pretty face strumpet

and be on her forefront

like a muffled horn

foreground

making music like nigga

somebody-

hand him a horn

blow boy blow

accomplished shit)

on the forefront

(blow boy blow)

on the forefront

(And the band played on.)

Miles & Coltrane: Blue (.)

The aura stills prevails.

Miles ahead-

      miles ahead

ahead by miles

Tribulations and trails

interpretations and styles.

So what if its all blues

or serpentine with

      blue in green.

Kind of blue by

drug induced delusions;

visionary or illusions,

from bebop

      to fusion,

electric dreams leaving

mental contusions.

Critics scream blasphemy

confusion strange

but you called it revolution.

                        Change.

This man with the horn

who every time he changed

his mind music was

                        Reborn.

jazz/rock/blues/

            you constantly changed the rules

and grew into a/ god

from the birth of cool

(ahead by miles;

        miles ahead

Miles & Coltrane: Blue (.)

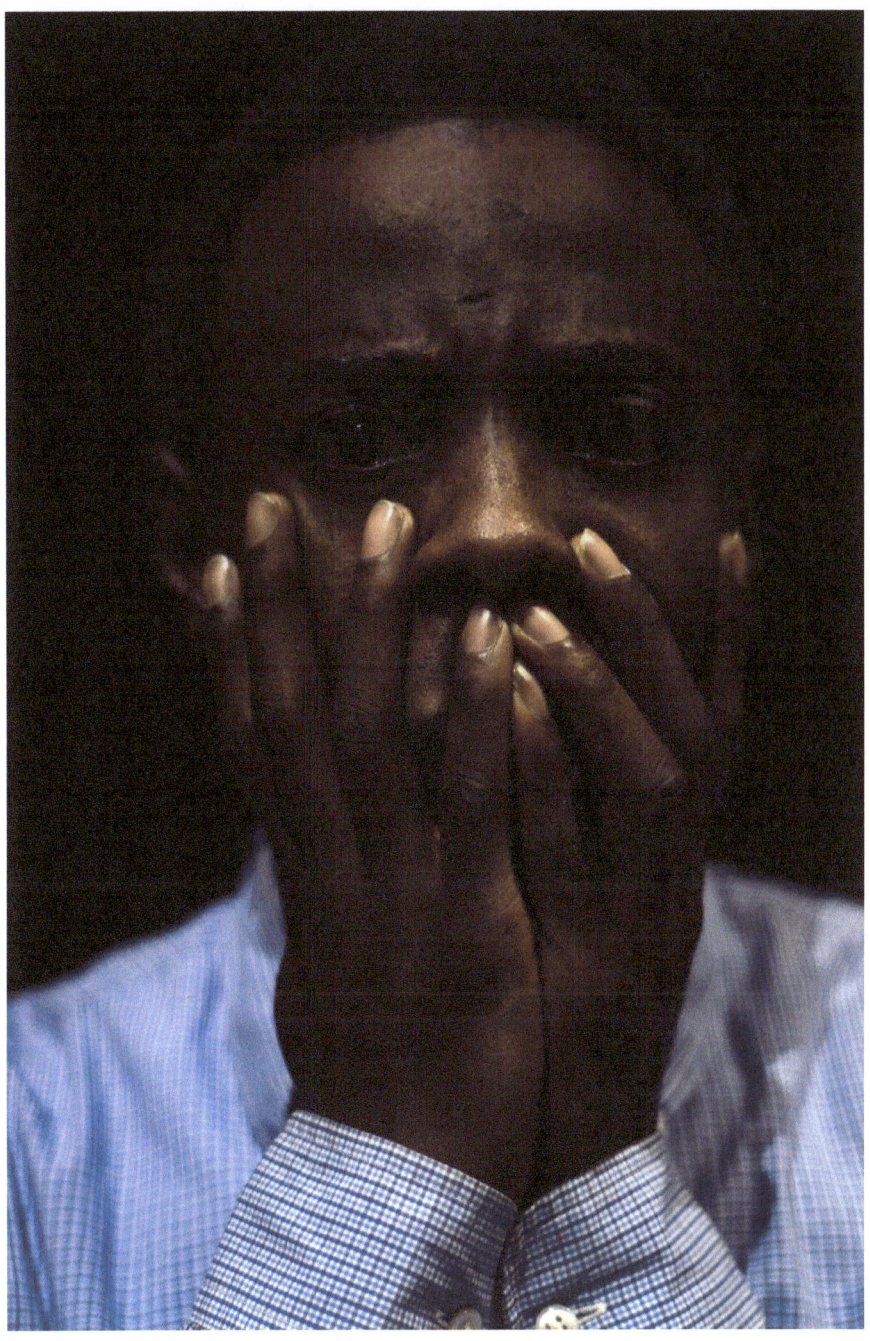

Miles & Coltrane: Blue (.)

on the corner

drawing sketches

of Spain with musical

notes in your brain

(Like E.S.P.)

in a silent way-

  from Tokyo to 600,000
  jammed tight at the Isles
  of Wright.

While many felt more
        at Filmore
  east
  and west
        even took seven steps
           to heaven
             to speak
               to Porgy
                 and Bess.

Chip on your shoulder, dressed to impress.
  Outlaw like Jack Johnson, your under arrest.

  For the journeys you took/us
upon miles/smiles

Miles & Coltrane: Blue (.)

as we listened/miles ahead as we
look/milestones behind;

press rewind.
We still find\that you were
ahead by miles ahead of your time;

but inside miles' head
    the demons fed,
on the hell bound,
running that voodoo down for Mr. Tutu,

while converting Stella by starlight;
his favorite valentine
use ta meet 'round midnight.

Our masculine beauty
    you drove women crazy
From miles in the sky
    you made us your water babies.

ever changing,
morphing into the black magus
the sorcerer loom to
have big fun with Nefertiti-
we felt the vapors from the bitches brew-
we be
    needy.

Straight
no chaser-
    as we took flight.
Waving bye-bye blackbird

soaring in a quiet night...

And we still need you like shadow needs a setting sun

Like future queens need future kings for future sons

   Someday our prince will come-

but the pain is as fresh as yesterday
even though its been since '91,
you're still the one.

to get up with that sixty years you held us
down

    with that horn
that sound
    so strong
so black
you had to turn your back.

profane.
precocious;

prolific/

profound,
political-

We sing your praises like a negro spiritual
I miss you miles

    We miss you....

Muthafucka I'm *still* here. Just play the tapes back. Muthafuckers always questioning the music. To them, the music is strange and changes so frequently. Well I'm alive and my experience constantly changes. Since I'm living why not imitate life. I'm always writing new chapters, though some conclusions aren't for sell. Therefore their lies secrets tucked away in my music, so the future will understand me.

Miles & Coltrane: Blue (.)

...Something new always)

   Accomplished shit

On the forefront

   Making music

        like nigga

He can always find something new

    Making music

(I can always find a new back up)

   Whether it was Coltrane
            Monk/Hancock

Coltrane

Something new always

(on the forefront)

Making music

Somebody hand him a horn

        (I can always find a new back up)

He can always find a new back up

Whether it was Coltrane
(caught a Coltrane to church)

Somebody hand him a horn
(Something new always...

This for me was Sunday prayer service. All I wanted to do was fill his presence through the room. Maybe they, the audience I mean; would find bit of peace, fury, salvation, like I did. Like I still do to this day. I sing praises the only way I know how, through the music. I needed the space to explore. I got the chance, took it and never looked back.

Throughout the eternal fabric of time

there have been those who thought they could,

those who wish they could,

those who fall victim to victimless failures.

Attempting to succeed through life without

succumbing to failures

(caught a Coltrane to church)

hell we all know the story

like the back of black calloused hands.

(hell we all know the story)

like the back of black/backbone;

kinfolk, cut me some of that smooth slack

from the back of black/backbone,

Miles & Coltrane: Blue (.)

connected to knee/bone-hip\jerk

                              -saxophone. dis-be-hard/work

whistling Dixie

especially when sweat

beating,

beading

    down

        forehead

like holy water blessing the dead.

Dammmmnnn cuzzzzz

be cutting through them notes/

like ghosts

gave him God

gave him grace/

give us that voodoo

that kinda of blue voodoo

bebopbedebododat

    yeah sometimes

        we needed it like that

God bring it back

    bebopbedebododat

        yeah now that's what

I call speaking in tongues. The spirit of

    a people can always and

Forever

in always

    and forever,

be found in

    foot to ground

Miles & Coltrane: Blue (.)

down home heaven

    holding my heavy

        heart like halleluiah's.

A love supreme saint sax-

at a news conference in Tokyo, Japan 1966,

a question was posed, where would you like to be

in ten years.

John William Coltrane replied,

"in ten years I would like to be a saint."

(caught a coldtrane to church)

in San Fran St. Johns African Orthodox Church

Alter stands black dread loc'd black jesus icon.

"in ten years I would like to be a Saint."

Eyes on a clutching saxophone clergy of men

with mouth mustering Sunday halleluiah notes

"in ten years".

Bishop becokoning "ya got to work for it,

the prayins in the playing"

                              "I'd like to be a saint."

I'm saying.

It might sound far fetched.

But bet,

The St. Johns in this church name didn't

come from biblical fame

but after John Coltrane.

Ask Gillespie.

Ask Coleman.

Ask Miles

How Trane

                      (see Trane's what they called him)

how trane took them on a ride.

With a-free-I-can.

    Sound scan.

        Sounds man,

    like those lungs

let loose a 'lil Asian influence

into that affluent.

Trane quit playing

that sound spiritual man

(Main tumse pyaar karti hun)

Caught a Coltrane to church)

That's right a spiritual man

    Said to be the first

major jazz

    musician mused

greatly infused

influenced by Indian music and cultured petri dish,

with a dash of ask 'Trane about eastern

philosophical studies

influencing his sound spiritual gifts from his

lips

"I've already been looking into those

approaches to music as in India in which particular

sounds and scales are intended to produce specific

emotional states."

                                                  (Trane talk to em')

Teach 'em

what them horns

won't explain from his

lips

"I would like to bring people something like

happiness. I would like to discover a method so that

if I want it to rain it will start away to rain."

(Caught a Coltrane to church)

Talk to 'em/teach 'em

what dem horns won't explain

from his lips

        "If one of my friends is ill, I'd like to

play a certain song and he would be cured, when he'd

        be broke, I'd bring out a different song and

immediately he'd receive all the money he needed."

(Caught a cold trane to church.)

Talk to 'em. Teach 'em.

(Main tumse pyaar karti hun.)

What dem horns won't explain.

Caught a

cold trane to church.

Talk to 'em. Teach 'em.

Main tumse pyaar karti hun.

What dem horns won't explain. Caught a

cold Trane to church.

A question was posed,

where would you like to be in

ten years? John William Coltrane replied,

    "in ten years I would like to be a saint."

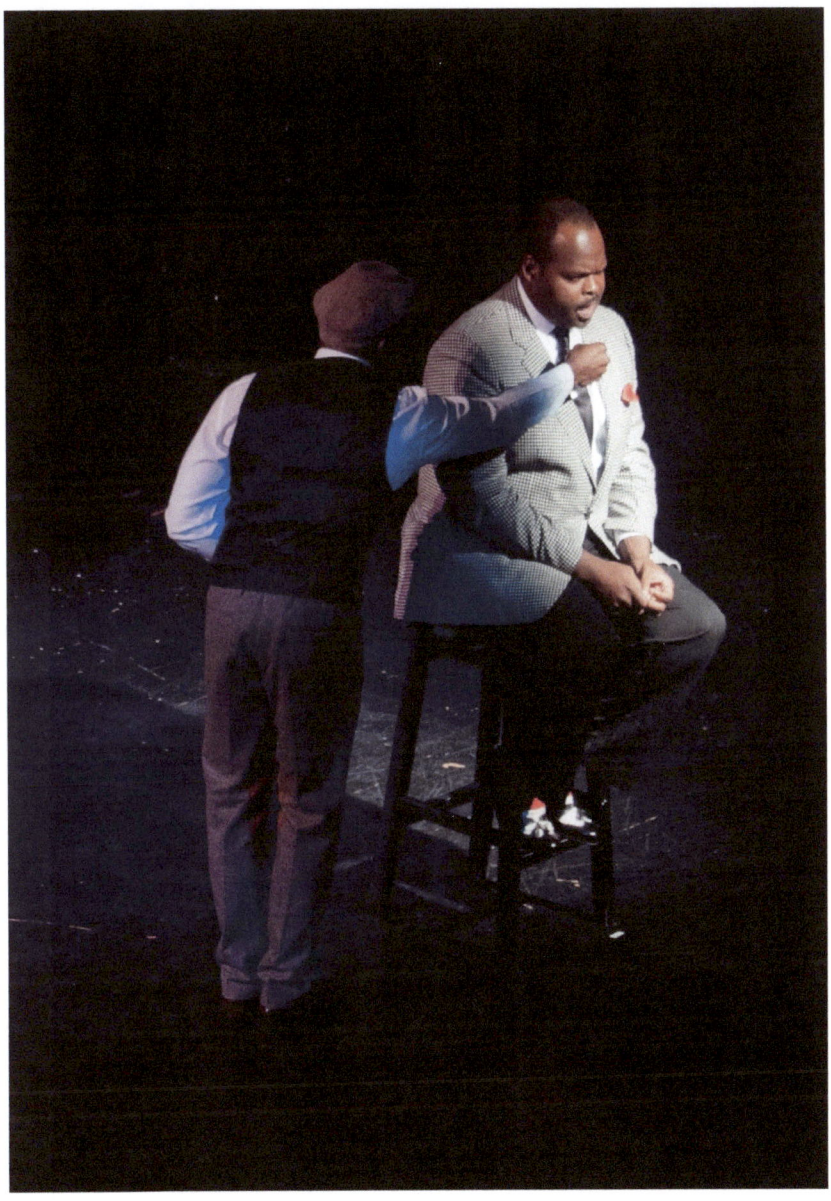

Ladies and gentlemen put your hands together

for the world renowned saint John

                                        ain't that cat cold Trane

Miles & Coltrane: Blue (.)

And there he sits a man

more a mentor

molded a building

from pebbles found in pavement

a man

who had a way

    with women

(a man)

who had a way

    with music

a man

who had a way

    with people

Man he was more

than a musician

more than an angel

more a god on earth

On the forefront

spike veins in vain with vain waste

sexy slim cutter with a pretty face strumpet

Blow boy blow

Music. Music. Music.

That's been the only constant in my life. Well, that and dope. Oh yes and women... But, mostly music. It was very important in my family.

My mother played piano and she used to love her records and so did I. The big thing back then was swing and I wanted to learn how to play that type of music. My mother always wanted me to play the violin.

Miles & Coltrane: Blue (.)

She thought it was respectable...

Yea, right, respectable...

  Ida of got my ass kicked everyday. Me, shiiiitttt, I wanted to play the trumpet. So Doc brought me one. I think he bought it to spite my mother. I was 12 and happier than a runaway slave. I loved that trumpet. Doc set it up so I'd get lessons from one of his old patients, Elwood Buchanan. Oh this muthafucker was tough but a very good teacher.

He'd say shit like, "don't come in here with that Henry James stuff boy". You don't need all the vibrato. Play it straight. He gave me confidence that made me want to work harder. Put raw rice or half peas in my mouth and spit them out one by one to get your lips use to playing the
trumpet. Ran everywhere i went to increase my wind.
it became an obsession.
I was in the high school band in Jr. high and had build quite a reputation around east St. Louis. So you know what that meant....

That's right... Pussy.

Irene. Irene Cawthon, we met in high school. She was a little older than me. Beautiful. We were the king and queen of Lincoln High School. So in love. In 1944 I graduated a semester early. Later that year, Irene gave birth to our first child. Yea I was a teenage dad, but a teenage dad on the move. Mother wanted us to get married, but fuck that, I was only 19 years old and i had just got accepted to the Julliard School of Music in New York City.

Concrete Generation

My mother wanted me to stay in east St. Louis. Shit, but as it turned out, Juilliard wasn't all it was cracked up to be. racist son of bitches.. i hate 'em.. a complete waste of time.

I remember one teacher in particular telling a bunch of students that the reason black people invented the blues was because we were so poor and sad. Hell, I felt
> compelled to raise my hand and tell her about my father and grandfather. How nobody in my family picked cotton, not even in slavery. How we were pretty well off and how we loved the blues. Well I guess I

pissed her off. cause i got a reprimanded. But, fuck it.

The bitch didn't know what she was talking about.

Anyway, I wind up quitting Juilliard. So here I am 20 years old. Started hanging out in the clubs gigging here and there making contacts, some good some bad. The good, shit. I was kickin it wit Bird, Diz, Billy Ecskine, some of the coolest, baddest cats in the world. And the bad, well that's where the dope came in.

1944 was the first time I shot heroin.

> Another trumpet player, Gene Ammons, gave it to me.

> Scott free. Free.
> > And I ain't been free since.

The dope changed me.
Changed me a lot. When I would
dry up, I had to do what I had to do to survive.
even if it meant pimpin'. Which is what i did.

I mean I could have been robbing, stealing, murdering.
so compared to that. Pimpin ain't so bad huh. and
it wasn't actually pimpin. See these women, whores,
prostitutes, call girls what have you.

   Well they wanted to take me out on a date and I would tell them, "Baby, i would love to go out on a a date with you, but i dont have any money". So they would give me two maybe three hundred dollars a piece a night.
Every night. So i stayed high.

I stayed high as hell.

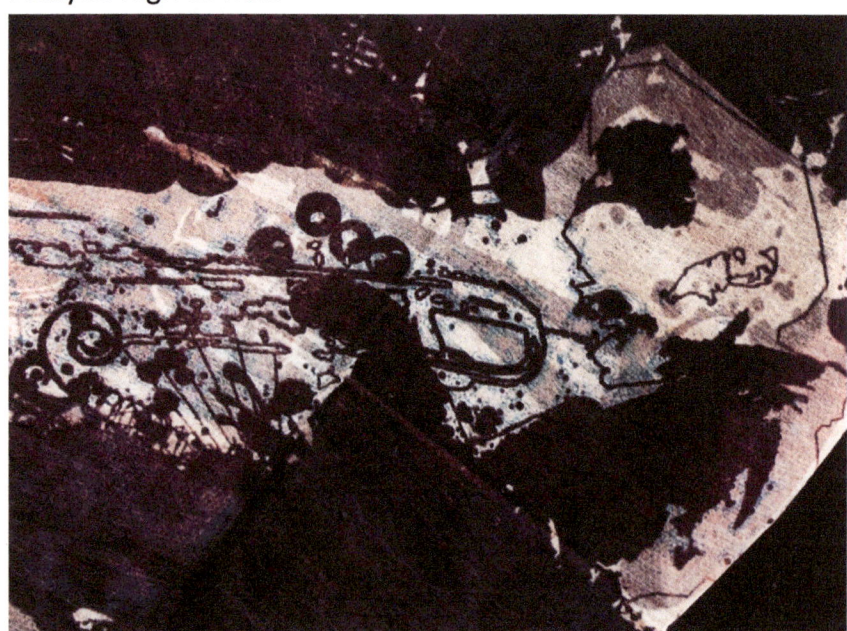

Concrete Generation

This was the best of times

The worst of times

he came into there lives in '49
this is when music was made

And lasted like forever
lasted where forever starts
this is high times

this is how he had
      'em believing that
         without him they'd
simply stop
    breathing

This was the best of times
the worst of times

    best of
This was the worst of times

    Set out again just to
Accomplish
    Something new always
        On the forefront

    always

Miles & Coltrane: Blue (.)

Concrete Generation

Don't ask me my name

Miles know my name,
Coltrane Know my name

These niggas-
these low brow pre
Madonna couldn't play
a kazoo if wasn't for me

Muthafuckas know my name

They get on stage and
got the nerve to play my songs

(cackle) like they made it
Like we aint sat in low-lit

      pissy bathrooms,
Comin' up with some
                far out shit, you know

Time traveling rhythms,
Gettin' ahead of our time
melodies,

We would get soo far gone.

to point of epiphany you
know?!

Then these muthaphuckas would fall asleep
                pass out...

Miles & Coltrane: Blue (.)

           lazy bastards
naw naw naw,
                they wont tell you my name
they wont give credit where is credit is due

Venus de Milo ... Mine

On the Corner...Mine
      So What...Mine

Blue Train...
           Mine Mine and Mine

Round Midnight?   ...Round Midnight was god damn
          genius.... A work of art

not fit for human ears
MINE!

they claim its all talent,

my ass

the real talent,
the real talent baby

is to get inside somebody

 and make music
make magic happen

Miles & Coltrane: Blue (.)

Hello I'm Miles Davis and im an addict

        Uh, my name is John William Coltrane, and I'm uh addict

Well kinda

        Kind of an addict

Kinda addicted, depending on how you see things
addiction isn't my problem, its why I do what I do

        addiction is where we all come from

where jazz comes from

        its where holding notes longer than your supposed to comes from

letting 'em go before they get too big

        like shootin stars burning out in the atmosphere

because addiction is the same thing as love….

        They jus call it addiction when they thinks its no longer healthy for you

but when you love something

        really love something… you need it
in your soul… in your heart

Miles & Coltrane: Blue (.)

                                            in your lungs, in your life

you need it in the bread you break

                                          you need it in your veins

in the bottom of glasses that don't get
empty

                              you take it with you and keep it

on the road

in your bed with all your sweat and your sin

in your thoughts

                                          its on your breath when

                                          you love something

you need it

All the time

all the goddamn

        time

                            a love supreme… a love supreme

but that's addiction

whether its heroin or

    liquor or women, or

                                          a love supreme

(Let music lull)

            even when it can't do you no more good

no goddamn good

                                      you still want it

still need it,

            but I've been addicted since long before I

        ever took my first warm shot of moonshine in

                      the back wood of Carolina

Miles & Coltrane: Blue (.)

before I ever learned of lust at age 13

        before anybody introduced me to horse

to that shit they call smack

        before I found the God, Allah through the prophet
                              Mohammed

I've been addicted as long as I can remember

            addiction is my first memory

(long pause)

listening to my mother play those black keys on

    our piano in east St. Louis

        my grandmother sang in our church choir and

Concrete Generation

        I remember her hitting those notes

those sweet as a muthafucker notes

        like outta everywhere I'd ever been I

        I belonged wherever them notes was

I was supposed to follow those notes wherever

they would take me

        and they was gonna follow me wherever I went

it was like meeting a part of you for the first time

        they was gonna follow me to Philadelphia

        then to Harlem then to Antibes, France

like knowing my black ass existed because on day I could make notes hum like Elwood Buchanan

Miles & Coltrane: Blue (.)

>   Coleman Hawkins, Lester Young

I've been addicted to those sweet ass notes as

long as I can remember people

>   as long as I can remember people,
>   I remember music

addiction is like a cycle

>   like 16 bars that won't let you go nowhere

like women leaving, then coming back

>   like forgiveness

like aggression

                              like taking the time to go as far as you
                    want with your instrument and you don't even have to
                                                               come back

ain't even gotta come back

                                                      yeah im addicted

                                                              to God

to women

                                                              to liquor

dominant 7th notes

                                                              to heroin

to heroin

                                                              modal

flatted 5ths

                                        im addicted to invention

to creation

                        To slow self destruction

Miles & Coltrane: Blue (.)

Miles & Coltrane: Blue (.)

Nothing more religious

Than this love supreme experience

Seven years of God exclaimed

Framed and exhaling it self in breath

through horns singing

rounded like my fingers

Over harp heart stringing

you notes to make these

days seem easier

fame don't always equal money

but honey you got sainthood circling

sheets of sound soon

to be pronounced

lift me baby

  I hear you transcending

Taal

     (rhythm)

Sanam

     (beloved)

Main tumse pyaar karti hun

               (I love you)

I locked you

in

For seven days you beat walls

Wailed hymns of waning addiction

Till apparitions were religion

Rhythm our star

struck patrimony

strings my sanctuary

that horn and u sexy

Miles & Coltrane: Blue (.)

Mr. Damn that Kat is more than cool

Cold

Dem Bold notes be
Blazin hotter than these
Summas in African-Americanized dashikis

Repatriation to rapturous spirit ancestry
Wrap me in notes like a sari

seeking
sanction in chanting

                      dreams to fruition

no need

for permission

African Orthodox Christian

We study Islam Hindu Yoruba

producing threes

                    MUSIC-DIVINITY-WE

Acheta Anata Govinda

                    CHANTING FOR PEACE

Miles & Coltrane: Blue (.)

Miles & Coltrane: Blue (.)

Concrete Generation

Dear Miles,

Momma always told me to play pretty; pretty like water droplets off the wings of angels. Pretty like her dress on Easter Sunday. I remember being in that boys band and she be up in the stands just a laughing and smiling; Like my horn came with an extra halo. My sister would stick her tongue out and I'd get all embarrassed in my white shirt and tie. They only wanted me to play pretty. I wanted to play like one of my Grandpa's Sunday sermons. Blow notes like they were hymns being sung to heaven.

I wanted to move people, like I was laying hands or something. I swear every time I place my lips upon that reed I can taste salvation. I now understand why Satan loved his reflection so much. Alice only wanted me to play for her. She would say play whatever, however, just make sure you play it for me. Deep down inside I wish I could play as pretty as she is play as pretty as she does my hands try to mimic the tapping of her fingertips upon my spine. I've always believed in angels I just never thought God would give me one.

Miles you use to say just play as long as you keep them crackers clapping we gonna be ok. You remember that time, you turned your back to the audience like you was telling them to kiss your ass. I know you was just trying to keep an eye on us. man you BAD! Its an anointing to play as pretty as you play.

But, now a days I dont feel so pretty since that thing gone got up in I cant even whistle right hands cant seem to stay steady got my heart pounding and I cant stop the sound of it calling my name. It exist in the parts of my vein where my music use to be its taking a toll on my love. In fact I think it stole my soul.

The other morning I woke up with a cut above my eye and I dont know what happened. Don't really care... All I know is that I need some more to survive to feel alive, to breathe. Been doing it so long, I dont even get high no more;

but Im getting better. Alice, been helping me break this thing and before long, we gonna be back together, cutting it up like the old days..

just wait for me..

I'll be there soon
(he can always find a new back up)

                                                      Sincerely, John

Miles & Coltrane: Blue (.)

                                      And I tried to kick

Two, three goddam times

                And when I finally kicked… really kicked, I
                          was 3,000 miles from home
                                    From my wife
                From the last place my horn felt comfortable

I know that feeling, like screaming in pain
And no one hears you cuz you yellin in the wrong
fuckin key

                By the time I kicked, I was drinkin 2 fifths of
                      bourbon a day to stop the trembling
                To stop the demons sneakin into my withdraw

I kicked once

Cold goddam turkey
Took me two weeks of shakin. Butt ass naked
Some Harlem hotel room
But I did it
Cleaned up. New suit. Got my old horn outta hock.
I was the most "back on the scene'nist" cat in the
city
(pause)
For 6 months

    Most people don't have the strength inside
              themselves to kick
    And most who've fallen that far from grace, can't see
           God trying to help them back up

Another time I kicked, I gave up horse and my
horn
Same time
5 longest motherfuckin years of my life
I never knew heroin without my horn being there
And I couldn't figure out which of them devils was
fuckin (with) me the most
So I told both of 'em to go to hell on the fastlane

    Can't see God pullin them outta hell one
        sobriety stair step at a time
    Cant see that that elixir is sin in syringes

But Me and God gotta agreement

    We don't know He doesn't condemn us
            Disown us

Sort of unspoken
But we both known he was gon let me get away with some shit

                He doesn't even mind that I'm addicted

As long as I stayed honest,

             As long as I stay addicted to the notes

True to the love of...

                   The reason he created me

 True to those sweet as a motherfucker notes

            Bringing the dream He had for me to life

As long as I stayed loyal to the seed He
planted
The day my father handed me that aluminum
Three keys and a mouthpiece

 And God said It was good

                    See God was a Jazz fan
          Long before Columbus found America
               Actually He's a horn player
    Since before we made reeds and melded brass to a tapered end
     God was Blowin breath of life into bodies of man

God knew, two men would make Blue

Miles & Coltrane: Blue (.)

Now some may call them
call girls
        hookers
prostitues
    hoes

though he loved each and
every one of the like

music
     like moonshine

like middle of the night
like I need to feel an itch
he loved them like

he loved like his music
He loved them like
they slipped in and out of
his life
like a needle

oh he loved them like music
like a half beat
like music

Miles & Coltrane: Blue (.)

A cappella thorn of perfectly
placed arrogance
resting on a half beat

Jazz colored rose with an aroma
that tunneled strumpets
saddled in his breath mutes
trumpet to trained

loose lips like a kiss he pushed a
wind storm through miles
of musical measures. The

trumpet trident felony fingers
 mimicking the trinity
Picasso of
        jazz paintbrush
                double dutch/man of two

faces most loved and
most hated highly de/baited by
critics 1960's antisocial/light

crowned prince of
darkness. No shuffling
of feet here

Davis is proud profile
misfit of an entertainer
he is a musicians playing
what's beyond notes

the abridged chord reeling in
coquetted flirting in allegro
tempo a scale out of
sequence ladies love to
climb ladies love my back to
the crowd style of quick sand

quick hands introducing
      modalism as theory
that had him robin womanhood
my funny valentine

in uncommon time catch a mile
Nefertiti he'll erase and redraw
sketches of Spain,

Amor martyr the restraints
there's a score of women
waist deep deeming him
opaque oh play some fusion

whose drunk off bebop
      forefront of blues renaissance
           he gave birth to cool
parker pick 'em one from the

chorus tree to go along
with Charlie staff lines line
my brew with bitches

get tipsy three times over
over cake baked with

blasphemy this trumpeter lived

for only two things:

femininity and a full set of
fermata creativity improv

to masterpiece playing what
he wanted wait and name

it later over dinner tabled
porgy with Bess
musical god altar of praise had him
without quiet night vexed with vibrato

America meet
    your blue black
hero God rose
    on the third day and
became a sanctified swagger

far from subtle shaking
ears intensely but softly
made love to your ears fears

b/c there's no mistakes
Miss take me home and get
psychedelic electric invent

a new kind of blue miss
wake and find me gone
rolling stone cold trane
trackline feed the beast
he stood on the corner with
"prove it to me" eyes full of

Miles & Coltrane: Blue (.)

whys full of style full
of shit miles smiles
the ladies say mmm

I'll date if he'll hug me
Playboy play your horn until Frances
leaves the west side story

to become a title in your
story dancing privately for
M.D. doctor hands up too

many tutus and Newport festivals
"You gots ta play a
long time to like yourself"

And oh, did he like himself
"ego only needs a good rhythm section" hide and seek a
percussion the sky

ain't the limit when creatin your
own shit and if they acting

too hip they can't play shit
shit Ferrari was an
extension of bravado bass

line something the strumpets
can sing to come at my
call whose drunk of bebop

now some may call
him a talented nigga
 some may call up an
uppity nigga
but you can call him god on earth

some misunderstand
those kind of children
that stick out when they younger

cause you see
he only knew how to

stick up for god
stick every woman he meet
you call him an uppity

nigga

making music like nigga

                                  It wasn't easy being me.

    Alton, Illinois, May the 25th Nineteen Hundred and Twenty Three. Miles Dewy Davis the Third. That's right the 3rd. Check my pedigree I come from a long line of exceptional cats. What polite white society would call uppity nigga. Doc told me. Hell, we didn't even have to pick cotton during slavery. Shit we was in the muthafucking house. Playing classical music for the Massa and his family.

Music liberated my family, it's in the bloodline. Yea the pedigree. Arkansas. My grandfather... my grandfather, Miles Davis was born round 1871. At least that's what our family bible said. Doc said he was the smartest man he ever knew. He was a bookkeeper. Worked for white folk. Made good money too. Shit he thought like white folk. Took his money and bought land. Then them crackers reminded him that he wasn't white folk and run him off his own goddamn land. And he couldn't do shit about it. Now that's some shit... some muthafucking shit.

    Anyway, my grand father still stayed in Arkansas. My daddy , Miles Davis. The second. My father was a dentist. They called him Doc and he had degrees from 3 universities including One from Northwestern. As a matter of fact all my aunts and uncles went to college. And that was kinda rare back in then for blacks. What do you call somebody who has 3 degrees? The same thing you call them when they're playin classical music on the plantation. Uppity niggas. should have been "a credit to my race". If we were really uppity, we woulda burned the damn plantation down. If we were really, really uppity we would have chased down them same crackers that ran my granddaddy off his land and shot them all in the fuckin head. We were uppity because we dared to dream, like them; and double dared to achieve it. When they looked at the Davis', they saw the promise of America and it scared the shit out off them. Back then white folks didn't know how to take you if your hand wasn't out. They wanted you begging or stealing.

it wasn't easy being me.
Uppity Nigga...

Miles & Coltrane: Blue (.)

every note

he ever played
    was a prayer
every air
that ever
    leaked from his lungs
was a prayer
 every note he ever played
was piece of heaven pulsing on the beat
every note he ever played
was a little piece of Nirvana
racing thru the notes
you ask Coleman
ask Gillespie
Ask Miles
every note was Sunday prayer service

Dear God,

This is how I pray.
    This is where it all started from.
Even then I didn't know why I did it.

I didn't know how
it made me feel like that.
I didn't know WHY I liked it.
But I liked it.

The rhythm.
The groove.
The message.

And I didn't have to say a word.
Just let my horn speak for me.
Speak through me.
I felt like You knew what I was trying to say.

Oh, Dear God,
This is how I pray.

Gems of good ol' GUT gospel music,
Buried at the bottom of each valve
Waiting for my spit to loosen them,
My fingers to dig them up and
My lips to blow them out
Oh, I never said it was pretty,
Just real.

And somehow, I just knew…knew…
You were bigger than this.
That You were out there somewhere,
waiting for me…

Showing me that when you play hide and go seek with the Creator,

The only way to lose
is to stop looking.
So I kept on playing
kept on praying...
Just let my horn search for me.
And oh, how I prayed.
Played like I shouldn't waste one drop of air in my lungs.

This, my sacrifice, my TITHE, meant more
Than any amount of dough I could put in some plate.
Man, I could hear You TALKING to me.

Your voice, a revolving system of locks and answers,
Always moving...
                always abounding...
                              always yearning to be

found.

Almost like a hidden code and the next note I prayed...

Held the key...
but only for a moment.

And sometimes that frustrated me.
Because You made me happy.
And I wanted to make others happy

So I just wanted to bring them You

                              -through me.
                   Just let my horn work for me.

Blast out a love for a Creator

who loved us enough to
make music,
You...
    are...
        MAJOR, man!

God, man, I know...
            I know You ain't in no needle.
        But...I
            ...I couldn't hear You.

They were screaming louder than You whispered.
                        And when they whispered,
You scream and now you sound
like them
When You were whispering and I wonder who's
                whispering, screaming,

So for a good minute, I pushed the plunger past the realm of possibilities
Only to find You still sitting at the helm of my proclivity to
Keep praying...
    playing...
        practicing...

Not so much for perfection, but for slightly above pontification,

Miles & Coltrane: Blue (.)

See, when I blow, I'm trying to play my way next to you.
See when I play,
    this (horn) becomes YOUR voice.
See, when I pray,
    your people hear You.

I look out and see they heads nodding and fingers snapping
And eyes closed but the only lips moving are mine
Because we in your presence and talking would be an insult

But You don't mind me breathing.
Oh, Dear God,
This is how I pray

  (I ain't never thought
about being no saint
'til now.)

This cat walks up to me and
says "You're my God!"
Can you believe that?
He put ME in YOUR position!

I told him not to call me that.
He can't call me that.
Only YOU can call people.

Miles & Coltrane: Blue (.)

So when you talk,
are you praying to me?
Is this (horn) how
I answer Your prayers?

Do I answer You loud enough?
Long enough?
He gave me plenty of space to work.

Play.
Pray.
Create.

We both talking to our demons.
Sometimes,
      he's calling his
           and I'm driving mine away
Sometimes,
      I'm calling mine
           and he driving his away.
Sometimes,
      I call it prayer
           and usually he don't care.

But he gives me plenty of space...
                                        To play.
                                        To pray.
                                        To create.

Plenty of space to try
        and become
                                          Holy.

Miles & Coltrane: Blue (.)

And it came to past that 2 men as different
 as night and day came together to
create the dawn of the future.

 One driven by the darkness of demons,
greatness spawned by an ego
that constantly needed to be relevant

who in the end his only sin
was that he wanted to be true to himself,
everything and everybody was just secondary.

The other always the angel in training,
trapped in this prison we call the flesh
he showed us that we need not verbalize prayers.

That the sax was a sacred voice box
that spoke of Hinduism, Judaism, Yoruba, African History,
Math, Science, Plato, Aristotle, Christianity,
He didn't play music, he played cosmic conversations with
God.

And they came to past. Miles Dewey Davis III September 28, 1991, Santa Monica, California at the age of 65. John William Coltrane, July 17th 1967 Philadelphia, Penn at the age of 40. But what they passed on to us was not just a body of music. But the skeleton for which music as we know it still changes, living and breathing today.

In their own way, they showed us through they're music, that in life the only thing that separates the here and now from the future, is not to repeat the past. So as we come to the present we realized both achieved what they wanted.

Miles you're still relevant in your music and in the spirit of your ego. You were both beauty and the beast, the complexity of Black Manhood.

John those conversations with God are a lot closer now and with your music you left us the entire blueprint to become saints.

As for the future of music,
well to quote Miles Davis
"just play the god damn tapes"

      listen closely and
          you can hear the
             future for it has
                already come to
                   past.....
                      thank you and goodnight.

Miles & Coltrane: Blue (.)

Finito.

ABOUT THE AUTHORS

Concrete Generation is a collective of artist based in Charlotte, NC, committed to the nurturing of imagination and advancement of cultural awareness through performance, visual and literary based art forms, and outreach workshop programs. Members of CG who co wrote the play Miles & Coltrane: Blue (.) include: Tavis Brunson, Norris Guest, Kendrea Griffith, Filmore Johnson, CP Maze, Carlos Robson, Miesha Rice, Boris Rogers and Quentin Talley. (@concretegenmag) www.concretegeneration.com

AFTERWORDS

The Making of Miles & Coltrane...

in Concrete...

Musings from the writers of Miles & Coltrane: Blue (.)

Miles & Coltrane: Blue (.)

Everything happens for a reason.

There are many beliefs, philosophies and religious systems that adhere to this same sentiment. I don't remember the very first time I heard this, maybe in a church somewhere. What I do remember about this phrase is that it fits perfectly with my involvement with the Miles and Coltrane: Blue (.).

To be perfectly honest, I don't recall when I was first approached to work on the project or if I was asked to write about Coltrane or if it was my choice. Prior to the invite the only thing I knew about John Coltrane was that he was a jazz musician. That's it. I couldn't name you one song by or one fact about the man. This you can thank to a pretty linear artistic childhood. I am, still in fact, learning about a lot of people who, since they weren't gospel artists, I'd never heard of.

So I did my research. I looked him up online and listened to some of his more popular music. I talked to people and asked questions about him. I picked the minds of some of the other CG artists working on the project about his relationship to Miles. From what I learned, I was so glad I got to write about John.

I related to him in so many ways. John Coltrane spoke directly to my soul through the dedication to his gift and his love for bringing life and love to people through it.

John had a desire to have a closer relationship to God, where he knew his gift came from. When I saw that people were so connected with him and his music to the point of wanting to make him a saint...and with me being a minister...my need to contribute to the project became abundantly clear.

I had a lot of fun with this project. As with a lot of my poetry, the initial draft came pretty fluidly. However, as most good writers know, the beast is in the editing. There are still times I will go back and read it and STILL want to change something! My goal in writing for Coltrane was to make sure that what people walked away with was more than the tortured Coltrane or the drug using Coltrane. I wanted people to understand Coltrane, the man of God. I wanted to give a voice to his music...to his life. Not just in the form of words that may fit into a song, but an actual voice. His voice.

And this is where "everything happens for a reason" comes into play for me. I realized toward the end of and after writing this piece, that Coltrane's relationship with Miles Davis in many ways mirrored my relationship with the other members of the Concrete Generation. I can directly relate to creating with someone that may not necessarily see eye to eye with my motives or everything I believe. The beauty is in the care that they have for me along with the respect for the passion of my writing.

Writing for this project helped me to appreciate these gifted, passionate and broken artists for what they really are...my friends.

They aren't perfect by any means. Neither am I. So it works...get it?

A prayer.

I hope this project does for you what it did for me. It is my prayer that you are as inspired, educated, uplifted, pissed off, and confused as I was and still am every time I see or read it. I pray it makes you see and learn something about yourself you never knew. My wish is that you see these two men, their music, and stories as those that changed the face of modern art (not just music) forever. Most importantly, I pray it brings you closer to whoever you call family and whoever you call God. I know it did for me.

It's been my pleasure serving you from the Master's Table. This is how I pray.

Tavis Brunson is a poet, minister, writer and playwright. Originally from Columbia, SC, he has performed and taught across the US. A national and regional poetry slam champion, he's also done many projects with Billy Graham ministries in Charlotte, NC. (@TavisBrunson)

Miles Davis! For me, the name itself conjures up the soundtrack of my life. So being asked to contribute to the writing of this play was a labor of love. To contribute to a play about a musical giant and it not be a musical was a huge challenge. When deciding to write, we the Generation all agreed that this would be more of a character study than a homage. These men were shaped by the times they lived in, warts and all. The intro to the show is of the utmost importance in describing this time period and also in the introduction of these two characters.

The sixties was a time when young Americans were rejecting the narratives of the status quo and began thinking for themselves. Being young, gifted, and black meant nothing compared to second class citizenship. The music was the blueprint for the human condition of the sixties and the muse for the tragically hip arc angels and demons on earth. The goal of introducing Miles to the audience is twofold. For those who know him we wanted to offer a reminder of the art of Miles. For those who are unaware, the intro is a lesson in the anthology of a pure genius. *Kind of Blue* is the epitomic example of Miles' brilliance; therefore I imagine the play being about those sessions.

Within the context of the play, I took it upon myself to be his voice. If his life was anything, it was complete. He experienced growing up in privilege, being a teenage dad, dropping out of Juilliard, pimpin', failed marriages, all this from his deepest melancholy to the heights of his ego.

Miles Davis proved to be one of the most complex musicians there was in entertainment. Who knew genius could be so brutal, so notorious? I wanted to reveal his character with honesty devoid of pretense. His character was one who refused to live the life of a second-class citizen, be it music, women or lifestyle.

Hell, if you let Miles tell it, he was the alpha and omega of music. He was the freest black man in America. The goal of the intro, and outro was to declare his (and Coltrane's) relevance is todays world.

Norris Guest is a native of Charlotte, NC and a proud father of 3 children. He is a founding member of Concrete Generation, SouthernFried Poetry Slam Champion and National Poetry Slam Semi-finalist with Respect da Mic Slam Poetry Team. Norris is currently working on a collection of poetry, prose and short stories, tentatively entitled, What's My Name?.

Miles & Coltrane: Blue (.)

Inspiration is fleeting; the "blessed ones" are the artist whose whole being exist within the mist of creation. When I first got the invite to write and perform for Miles & Coltrane: Blue(.), I was already a jazz fan. In fact, I have an affinity for most music. As a writer, I've always been drawn to great lyrics, however, since most jazz songs are void of words, therefore, I was not overly excited by the project, at first. Then I began deeply listening to the music, and researching the history. I started to understand the passion that lives within each note. The thing about passion is that it will never be boxed in and defined by genres, regions, or even skin color. Once passion is brewed within the belly of the artist it must come out.

As an artist I am called to write as these men were called to music. My favorite jazz song is "Naima" by John Coltrane. Each note falls like rain drops, quenching any soul daring enough to listen. The essence of Coltrane's music is reminiscent of testimony. I believe that we are more spiritual creatures than mere men. Coltrane's "A Love Supreme" reflects such testimony seemingly without effort. In this he piece offers more than just music. The music of Miles is so brash, unapologetic, and yet the two artist showed the world that being human is a struggle between being great and giving reverence to the God that exist within us.

Miles & Coltrane: Blue(.) is the timeless tale of man's constant battle between the angels that inspire, and the demons that bind. Somehow, artists tend to find a way to create great beauty within the chaos we call life.

This play is not only about two musical pioneers but it is also a telling of how art and music comes to be. The art of these men is likened to Monet's recounting the moments before and after painting 'vanilla skies'. Art is the reflection of the lives we live. Miles Davis knew this, John Coltrane knew this, and because of the retelling of a timeless friendship, THE WHOLE WORLD SHALL KNOW.

Filmore Johnson has been writing and performing spoken word poetry for over 10 years. 2-time regional poetry slam champion. Co-wrote and acts in the play Miles & Coltrane: Blue (.), but he is more than just a mere poet. His ability to sing and lyric writing is something that sets him apart from many of his counterparts. (@TheRealFilmore)

In the first half you get to know roots of what made both of these men so determine to play their horns and to be respected as men. The second half you learn what made them legendary, the obstacles of addiction, and the life they came to create Blue. In one of John's cold turkey attempts, Alice locked him in a room for seven days at his request. This is a scene Q chose to open the second scene with and I've always thought that was a brilliant transition especially because I'm in it!

Taal Sanaam: The poem personifies the depth of black love and healing power of music that Alice and John Coltrane both believed in. I chose to write from the perspective of Alice Coltrane because the story of the black female is so seldom heard. Also I've always been fascinated by the women behind strong men. Most importantly I wanted to show a contrast between Coltrane and Miles with relation women.

Every time I pull on that blue and white dress to become Alice I reflect on the research and writing process, which began in 2006. I had no way of knowing then that Creating and sharing Miles & Coltrane would be the most enriching experience of my artistic career. Together we've gone from collaborating at the "art house" to opening night in New York to sharing a flat in Scotland and selling out at the Jazz Bar. It has been worth all the hardships related to producing an independent project. This has never felt like work, it felt more like an ongoing conversation with friends.

Now, this conversation has spread internationally and like Jazz, it's always evolving.

It amazes me that there are so few works on Miles Davis or John Coltrane. As an artist I feel I am paying homage to two men who changed the face of music. As a member of Concrete Generation I hope that we can have a fraction of the impact that these two men have had on countless lives.

Quotes to remember from our travels with the show "MORE WORDS!" "Please don't be the beat".

Kendrea Griffith is a poet, writer and multimedia journalist. She has released two albums of poetry and music, published a book, and her writing has been featured on both stage and screen. She holds a Master of Arts in New Media Journalism, owns and manages the popular InTheseStreets! Blog, and makes a living as a journalist, multimedia designer and internet marketing consultant. (@mektxt)

Miles & Coltrane: Blue (.)

This project is a culmination of artists with so many varying art forms. All of us were born in different states, and some in different countries. Yet somehow, someway we all ended up in the same city. Ironically that's where the cliché being at the right place at the right time comes from. Painters, musicians, graphic artists, writers, photographers, fashion designers, actors, singers, dancers, immigrants and dreamers: a Concrete Generation. Whether it is the Fringe Festival debut in Scotland or The Spoleto Festival in Charleston, South Carolina I think about the randomness that birthed this play and all of the strange places it has taken me up until this point.

No matter the city, state, or venue no show is exactly the same. The artistic anarchy that is Concrete adds a little excitement and a lot fun into each performance. One bit of variety to the play is where I'm given leeway to freestyle verses in between the monologues of Miles and Coltrane and Heroine. There were times where Filmore or I were unable to make a performance so we would have to perform both our parts, or have commitments a few cities away and racing to get back by time the house lights go down! Sometimes the antics happen before a show.

One day before the cast was due to set off and fly to Scotland for the Fringe Festival, Q's doing some last minute dotting of the "i's" and crossing of the "t's" to be sure all of us were able to travel.

When I asked Q how are things looking, he lets out an extremely long sigh and explains to me that due to the way the tickets were priced along with our extremely small budget, one of us was going to have to fly into London solo, instead of flying straight into Edinburgh, with the rest of the group. He figures that since I'm once a Marine always a Marine I can handle it, I figure since I've forgotten most of the cities I've been in overseas than I can remember he's right, so naturally I've been deemed the chosen one.

Charles Daniel Perry Jr. is commonly known throughout the literary world and performance arts community as CP Maze. A highly decorated United States Marine Corps Veteran, a published author, a former 3rd & 4th in the world ranked performance poet, and Cofounder of Concrete Generation; CP Maze's passion, creativity, and awe inspiring delivery has history booked him as a prominent artist of our time. (@CPMaze)

Miles & Coltrane: Blue (.)

My Little Ripple in This Masterpiece..

The conception of the idea for this play was highly nurtured, revered, and most importantly favored. I remember it being placed on the table of our creative minds, a mere vision greater than anyone of us could have ever imagined. We all had already possessed the passion for writing therefore it was no problem putting those passions to work. It was a carefree fusion of minds: one free weekend, an apartment, and a handful genius minds. A few days and red solo cups later, we had more than a skeleton for the masterpiece before the world today.

As a female writer, I was assigned to write from the perspective of Miles' rendezvous with women and how it shaped, hindered, and inspired his career. After researching his tumultuous encounters with women, frankly, it was difficult to accept Miles' seemingly careless demeanor, but I welcomed the challenge. It allowed me to capture the essence of an amazing musician from a controversial perspective. I approached it as a stream of consciousness; a constant, sometimes, complicated string of thoughts. My addition to the overall play remained that way in the final version, idiosyncratic and unrestrained, in order to capture Miles' nature. Reading back on it, it is probably one of my most prized pieces. It shows a love for language that I sometimes forget, a love that can be muted by mainstream audiences. For that, it remains a piece I'll forever marvel.

The first time I got to perform live with the cast, not only was I thrilled by the stage, I couldn't believe how simplistically intricate it had become. Even more important, it was fulfilling to have watched it go from idea to full production.

I am honored to be amongst such talented people; people who are both marvelous artists and amiable personalities off stage.

Miesha "Ocean" Rice: This mother and Charlotte native holds a B.A. and M.A. in English Literature. A writer/performer/teacher for over a decade, released 3 independent albums, ranked 4th at the WoWps, and competed in/with several slam teams/competitions on both coasts.

Miles & Coltrane: Blue (.)

For the life of me I can't remember a single present I received for Christmas that year except for one gift from my cousin Scott. Scott was the cool older cousin who always had a convertible and a girlfriend, which to me was a big deal. I still wonder what inspired him to buy me, his immature eleven-year-old cousin three CDs labeled 'the Miles Davis Collection.' With time, I would fall in love with each of them. 'In A Silent Way,' is a hauntingly subtle album that grows in scope as it unfolds, 'Sketches of Spain,' is a flirtatious and exotic recording that over the years has become my favorite of Miles' albums, and 'Kind of Blue,' was the object of my first jazz obsession. "You'll like that." Scott said when I looked to him for a reason as to why this constituted a Christmas gift. I was used to Huffy bikes and cash for Christmas, what was I supposed to do with jazz music? Driving the six hundred miles back to our home in North Carolina the next week, I decided to try out this Miles Davis guy. I started with 'Kind of Blue,' and twenty minutes later when we pulled into a Wendy's for lunch, I was still waiting for somebody to start singing.

At twelve I changed schools. Summit Charter School was a strange new place. Equally strange was our assistant teacher, a theatrical, gregarious, 'Seinfeld'-addicted young guy named John Jeter. Mr. Jeter was a George Clinton, Willie Nelson and Nirvana kinda guy. He knew everything about music. He told us about the last time Paul McCartney visited John Lennon, and what Thelonious Monk thought of Miles Davis' later work.

He told us about how he first heard that his friend had passed away minutes before hearing Al Green sing the BeeGee's "How Can You Mend A Broken Heart?" Even after I started high school, I'd still come back to get Mr. Jeter's opinion and guidance. One day, he said "I've got something you'll dig, Robson." before revealing a full sized suitcase packed with CDs and books. "Keep it as long as you need to, just don't lose my shit." I was in heaven, copying CDs night and day. Bob Marley, Sly and the Family Stone, the best of Stax Records, BB King. Along with the music came books. Most of them I looked at but never got into, the one exception was Miles' autobiography. I almost read it cover to cover before I gave it back. I didn't finish it because I didn't want it to end.

Miles kept it pretty honest in his book and I loved him for it. It was all unadulterated, his music, his addictions, his language, his actions. Years later, Norris Guest, another writer on this project and I agreed that we hated when people claimed to 'get' Miles Davis. Miles was light years ahead of most of the musicians he worked with and every asshole that's bought a Miles album since claims they 'get' him. We've decided that you can't 'get' Miles music, so much as you 'get' to be close to it.

When I got to college I found myself writing and performing with 'poets,' I wasn't much of a poet however, I was more a storyteller.

And this project has been a culmination of my two favorite things, music and storytelling. Quentin, or "Q" as we call him, cast me in a play once with Sultan Omar El-Amin who was already my favorite actor in the city. Standing in the back of the theater one night I promised myself that one day I'd write something for Omar. Less than a year later we were in rehearsal for this show. On opening night, I stood backstage listening to Omar and Q play Miles and John and cried when they came to the scene I'd written. For some of us, this show is a dream come true. I'd love to keep bragging on how great the people I've worked with on this project are but you'll see that once the curtains go up. What I will say is this. Good music is universal, it is the way God reminds us of things too holy for words, and I am a Miles Davis kinda guy. It was an honor trying to tell his story. I won't claim to get him, but I sure as hell dig him. Just like Scott and Mr. Jeter said I would.

Carlos Robson is a performance poet, playwright, and teaching artist. A two time National Poetry Slam champion, he has performed throughout the U.S. and Canada and is currently working on a new play about American immigration entitled "Free + Brave." (@Carlosthepoet)

Miles & Coltrane: Blue (.)

When I look back at this process, this journey we all decided to embark on together. I don't think we had any idea of what we were going to accomplish. We just saw another chance to express ourselves. This was also chance to present our passion for words and theater. We mixed that passion with our admiration and love for the minds and talents of Miles and Coltrane.

This journey, still on going, has been incredible and literally lead across the world with more to come. Now, if I were to reflect specifically on my contribution to this inspiring work, then I would have to say that process of writing for Heroin was dark and revealing. I wanted the audience to gather the understanding of what this drug meant to these men, albeit from our perspective. At times it was as important as the music itself. Heroin became the notes, the creation, the rise, the fall, and a muse, if they allowed it to be.

I was trying to personify Heroin as the 3rd member in this otherwise magnificent duo of Jazz greats. I'll admit to taking some assumptions as to what the voice of Heroin would sound like. I tried to imagine having grit and bite, attitude and contempt for the musicians because they tried to hide its influence and presence in their lives and music. It was beautiful challenge but yet an important voice to the play.

I was honored to have written it and even more humbled to be apart of this journey with these amazing writers.

Boris "Bluz" Rogers is an Emmy award winning Host, Poet, Actor, and Playwright. Bluz has been performing spoken word and hosting events for 8 years. An active member in the community, Bluz has worked on several projects with organizations such Blumenthal Performing Arts Center, CBS Radio, Radio Disney, ESPN, and NASCAR. (@MrBluz)

Miles & Coltrane: Blue (.)

As in jazz, there are many layers, various vamps and bridges in the story of the making of Miles & Coltrane. So let the sessions begin...

Musicians, visual artist, poets and any other form you could think of were my closest friends, most of which lived in the North Davidson street Arts District. We had late night writing and jam sessions while trading philosophies and spirits until the sun came up. It was amazing to be apart of an arts community that was mind blowingly talented and passionate about their craft. This arts district was (and still is) the stomping ground for the Concrete Generation.

The play began as a mere conversation on the back steps of our regular poetry spot back in late summer 2006. Corey McClure, a band leader and I were having our ritual mid show smoke and were catching up on life and art. Somehow the conversation led to music and jazz in particular. Corey said, "do u know of any shows that surround Miles Davis & John Coltrane. They are the two biggest jazz artists and I don't know if their stories have ever been told." I thought long and hard about it and realized there weren't any shows (at least that I knew of) like that. I told Corey, "we should work on it." We rapped some more and throughout the conversation we dreamed of a show and it evolved from a straight up concert vibe to adding poets in to write the script and perform.

By the time the conversation was over and since most of the crew were in the building that night, in less than a min, I was walking up to poets saying we are going to write a play. That's how the idea came about. Now came time to put it into action.

We had had a couple meetings about the script, to talk approach, and most just started writing and handing me their work. But by this time, we were all swamped with life, paying bills and such; and I had caught the theatre bug again. I had done a couple of shows in Charlotte, while I was doing poetry, but I wasn't seeing any shows that represented the diverse black canon of American Theater.

So I started, On Q Productions (now On Q Performing Arts) focusing on classic, contemporary and original works about the black experience; We were starting to get some buzz with our first shows in late 2006, In The Blood by Suzan Lori-Parks, Day of Absence by Douglas Turner Ward and For Colored Girls by Ntozake Shange. So that took up a lot of my time. All this was going on while Miles & Coltrane was on the back burner, simmering. In 2008 Slam Charlotte was on it way to winning its 2nd National Poetry Slam Championship. CP Maze and L Boogie and I all moved into a house together, affectionately named 'The ArtHouse.' This is where many artist from out of town and in town alike came to hangout and create. The ArtHouse was also where a vital part of the art scene continued to evolve and thus this show.

With my focus back split between poetry and theater, it was time to pick up Miles & Coltrane again. Once I began to edit the pieces given to me, I quickly realized we had something great going on. After consulting with everyone on what they wrote, it was time to reach out to other members of Concrete and ask them to add to pieces, for at that point, we had only had about 30 minutes of a script. We all had writing assignments to bring the piece together thematically. Oh what a job they did!

I'll never forget when all the pieces were put together. I sat in my room at the ArtHouse and begin to edit the script. I was concerned that the edit was going to be tough since the show was comprised of multiple voices/authors.

Although we held some meetings as a group, we didn't write together in the conventional sense. We all wrote on our own time over the course of two years. When looking at what everyone had wrote, it was like we were all on the same page. I couldn't believe it. Everyone had put there heart and soul into these pieces. It was at that point I knew within my heart we had a certified hit. We wouldn't find out until we put it in front of an audience. But, before history could be made, I needed to finish the script. I dissected the script into parts and formed characters and ambience for the show. While continuing to edit I began to reach out to those artist and friends I knew would be performing in the show.

I went back to Corey and told him we now have a script to work with; lets get the band together! Corey is a talented, humble musician and he felt there were better suited jazz musicians in the city. Corey recommended a mutual friend, Stephen Gordon. Stephen was another young cat around the scene, had grown up in Charlotte and was known for his genius musical skills. I hit him up and he quickly became our Musical Director for the show. He knows some of the baddest jazz musicians in the nation and keeps the show sounding crispy every time. Once we spoke about the role the band, it has been interesting watching the show evolve with regards to the music.

The band doesn't "play" Miles & Coltrane tunes, well sometimes they do, but the music is always progressive and composed on the spot, complementing the mood of the dialogue and at other times straight shedding. The band has been a trio, quartet, quintet, sextet, electric, straight ahead, acoustic, hip hop infused and everything in between.

Once the band was on board, I hit up other artist in the community, starting with Marcus Kiser and Wolly Vinyl, who were the graphic designers of the murals of Miles & Coltrane used as the backdrop for the set. Then I reached out to two professional ballet dancers, Jhe Russell and Randolph Ward, who played Coltrane and Miles respectively.

These then members of The North Carolina Dance Theater would be the perfect fit to portray them in movement. Unfortunately, both of them moved on to dance companies in Europe. The show has a totally different feel without the dance movement aspect. This is just another example of the continuing evolution of the production.

During the process of editing, I had already reached out to Sultan Omar El-Amin, a company member of On Q and my brother in the arts. Actually scratch that, just my brother. Omar is an amazing actor. He is absolutely electric on stage. Omar had been in all the On Q shows thus far. He and I would hang out and dream about a sustainable life in the arts. After directing him in various roles, I knew he would 'put his foot' into the character of Miles. Once he did his research and asked questions, overtime the resemblance to Miles became uncanny. Nowadays he goes into character about an hour before the show, talking shit to everybody, you'd think you were talking to Miles Davis himself. Omar is Miles Davis.

I decided that I wanted to play Coltrane. While researching the show, I felt a real connection to Coltrane and his philosophies. Like me, he was raised in the south and in the church. He was so passionate about his craft, as I am. Also, since I hadn't acted, as much as I would like, due to responsibilities of being a producer/artistic director of a company, so I figured this was my chance.

Then next, some of the writers would play characters in the show. I wanted Maze and Filmore to be the narrators. Their styles complement each other and reflect the ying and yang personalities that were Miles and Coltrane. Mekkah would play Alice Coltrane, her poem showed the spiritually in Coltrane's music. Plus we badly needed some female energy in such a male heavy show. With this in mind, Miesha recorded her poem and was able to perform a couple of times with the show. I talked to Swan, who has a great voice and knew she'd be awesome as the vocalist for the show. And Carlos, would come in as Heroin.

Now that the show and cast was formed it was time to perform. Our first show was in April of 2008 at Duke Energy Theater at Spirit Square. Everyone was nervous, for we had put in 2 long years writing the show and it would suck if people didn't like it. At the end of the night the audience of about 50 or so was on there feet and applauding. Afterwards, folks kept telling us how much they enjoyed the show and that we had something very special. I agreed, and so did the rest of the crew.

We began to push the show. It was being developed and produced under the On Q umbrella, so we would fit in a one night only show here and there over the next year. In 2009, we made the decision to head to Edinburgh Fringe Festival to gain international attention.

First, we premiered at E59 Theater in NYC for their, East to Edinburgh Festival and received standing ovations every night. This solidified that we had not just a good show but a great show on our hands. As a theater kid, I always knew that if you can make it in New York (even if only for a little while), you can make it anywhere. A month later we were in Edinburgh. We did well and had a great time at the fringe; but at the end of the day the impact was only a splash in a sea of shows. We were only able to go for a week and only able to take a third of the cast. So we continued to push. Next we would further develop the show in Charlotte, with a couple of one night only performances and during CIAA. Then we went back on the road, performing at 14th St Playhouse in Atlanta during the National Black Arts Festival, Studio Theater at the DC Black Theater Festival, and Piccolo Spoleto Festival in Charleston.

One of the main hindrances of the show, really the only one, is that we had no money backing us. We had plenty of support, just not enough money. I was producing the show, and as a full time artist, my pockets were not as deep as I'd like. As artists, we still kept pushing and continued to gain more and more audiences members and acclaim for our labor of love. Thankfully we have come full circle and now the show is out on it own with great co-producers on our team now, Rick Lazes and Tammy Greene. This show really is the spirit of a community coming together to support the arts.

From the artist themselves mentioned earlier to individuals like; Chris Dennis, Valaida Fullwood, Tracy Russ, James Bazzelle, Morenga Hunt, John Moore, Geraldine Sumpter, Paul Sires and Ruth Ava Lyons, Dr. Tom Hanchett and Carol Sawyer, Jumanee and Sagg Torrence, JC, Tom Gabbard, to the institutions; The Gantt Center, Blumenthal Performing Arts, NC Dance Theater, Mint Museum, Arts and Science Council, Foundation for the Carolinas to organizations like Touch One Productions, Slam Charlotte, Respect The Mic, Dupp & Swat, and to all the audience members who have come to the show over the past 5 years; this show would not have been possible without you. Therefore you are all producers in my eyes.

One of the reasons this production has been so successful thus far is the shows ability have something new on the forefront. The show changes constantly but somehow stays the same. All the artists involved with this project have evolved from being more than acquaintances but dear friends and more importantly, family. The evidence is when we are performing the piece, we all listen to each other and can feel each other's rhythm. Therefore the show is never the same twice. Truth be told, we've only "rehearsed" the show once. All of these talented artists just come together and have a conversation between each other. Just like Corey and I had on the back steps of the poetry spot.

Quentin Talley is an actor, poet, director and producer. He is Founder and Artistic Director of On Q Performing Arts in Charlotte, NC. He is the 2012 recipient of Theater Communications Group LeadershipU fellowship, funded by the Andrew Mellon Foundation. He is currently working with his mentor and host theater, Lou Bellamy & Penumbra Theater Company. (@QuentinTalley)

PHOTO APPENDIX

pg. v – Miles Davis, designed by Wolly Vinyl (God City Art Collective)

pg. vi – John Coltrane, designed by Marcus Kiser (God City Art Collective)

pg. 9 – left to right: Charles Perry Jr. as The Storyteller, Filmore Johnson as The Griot, McGlohon Theater at Spirit Square, Charlotte, NC June 2009 | photo by Lovo

pg. 12 – left to right:: Samuel Luther Allison –piano, Eleazar Shafer –trumpet, Tim Scott Jr. – drums, Tim Singh –Bass, Marcus Jones –Saxophone @ Duke Energy Theater at Spirit Square, Charlotte NC June 2013 | photo by Lovo

pg. 13 – Sultan Omar El-Amin as Miles Davis, Booth Playhouse, Charlotte, NC Nov 2008 | photo by Lovo

pg. 14 – Quentin Talley as John Coltrane, Booth Playhouse, Charlotte, NC Nov 2008 | photo by Lovo

pg. 19 – Eleazar Shafer – Trumpet | photo by Lovo

pg. 20 – Sultan Omar El-Amin as Miles Davis | photo by Gena J.

pg. 21 – left to right: Filmore Johnson as The Griot, Sultan Omar El-Amin as Miles Davis, Samuel Luther Allison -piano, Charles Perry Jr. as The Storyteller | photo by Lovo

pg. 25 – left to right: Samuel Luther Allison –piano, Eleazar Shafer –trumpet, Tim Scott Jr. – drums, Tim Singh –Bass, Duke Energy Theater at Spirit Square, Charlotte NC June 2013 | photo by Lovo

pg. 26 - Sultan Omar El-Amin as Miles Davis , Duke Energy Theater at Spirit Square, Charlotte NC June 2013 | photo by Lovo

pg. 28 - left to right:: Samuel Luther Allison –piano, Tim Scott Jr. – drums, Tim Singh –Bass, Marcus Jones –Saxophone @ Duke Energy Theater at Spirit Square, Charlotte NC June 2013 | photo by Lovo

pg. 29 – Marcus Jones- Saxophone, Charlotte NC June 2013 | photo by Lovo pg. 34- left to right:: Filmore Johnson as The Griot, Quentin Talley as John Coltrane @ Duke Energy Theater at Spirit Square, Charlotte NC June 2013 | photo by Lovo

pg. 35 - left to right: Tim Singh –Bass, Marcus Jones –Saxophone, Duke Energy Theater at Spirit Square, Charlotte NC June 2013 | photo by Lovo

pg. 36 - left to right: Jhe Russell as John Coltrane (always trying to elevate), Phillip Wack – Saxophone, Booth Playhouse, Charlotte, NC Nov 2008 | photo by Lovo

pg. 41 - left to right: Stephen Gordon –drums, Quentin Talley as John Coltrane, East to Edinburgh Festival, E 59 Theater, NYC 2009 | photo by Lovo

pg. 42 - left to right: Filmore Johnson as The Griot, Quentin Talley as John Coltrane, Duke Energy Theater at Spirit Square, Charlotte NC June 2013 | photo by Lovo

pg. 44 - Sultan Omar El-Amin as Miles Davis , Duke Energy Theater at Spirit Square, Charlotte NC June 2013 | photo by Lovo

pg. 45 - Sultan Omar El-Amin as Miles Davis , Duke Energy Theater at Spirit Square, Charlotte NC June 2013 | photo by Lovo

pg. 46 - Sultan Omar El-Amin as Miles Davis , Duke Energy Theater at Spirit Square, Charlotte NC June 2013 | photo by Lovo

pg. 49 – Miles Mural by Wolly Vinyl | photo by Lovo

pg. 51 – Carlos Robson as Heroin, McGlohon Theater at Spirit Square, Charlotte, NC June 2009 | photo by Lovo

pg. 54 – (top pic) left to right: Sultan Omar El-Amin as Miles Davis, Samuel Luther Allison –piano, Tim Scott Jr. – drums, Tim Singh –Bass, Carlos Robson as Heroin, Quentin Talley as John Coltrane, Duke Energy Theater at Spirit Square, Charlotte NC June 2013 | photo by Lovo

pg. 54 – (bottom pic) Carlos Robson as Heroin, East to Edinburgh Festival, E 59 Theater, NYC 2009 | photo by Lovo pg. 56 - Quentin Talley as John Coltrane, Duke Energy Theater at Spirit Square, Charlotte NC June 2013 | photo by Lovo

pg. 63 - (top pic) left to right:: John Colliani –piano, Sultan Omar El-Amin as Miles Davis, Gray –bass, Quentin Talley as John Coltrane, Stephen Gordon –drums, East to Edinburgh Festival, E 59 Theater, NYC 2009 | photo by Lovo

pg. 63 – (bottom pic) left to right: Jonny Fung –piano, left to right: Sultan Omar El-Amin as Miles Davis, Charles Perry Jr. as the storyteller, Filmore Johnson as The Griot Tim Scott Jr. – drums, Quentin Talley as John Coltrane, Tim Singh –Bass, Duke Energy Theater at Spirit Square, Charlotte NC June 2013 | photo by Lovo

pg. 64 – (top pic) left to right: Sultan Omar El-Amin as Miles Davis, Charles Perry Jr. as the storyteller, Filmore Johnson as The Griot, Quentin Talley as John Coltrane, Duke Energy Theater at Spirit Square, Charlotte NC June 2013 | photo by Lovo

pg. 64 – (bottom page) left to right: Eleazar Shafer –Trumpet, Tim Scott Jr. – drums, Marcus Jones –Saxophone, Duke Energy Theater at Spirit Square, Charlotte NC June 2013 | photo by Lovo

pg. 65 - Tim Singh –Bass, Duke Energy Theater at Spirit Square, Charlotte NC June 2013 | photo by Lovo

pg. 66 – Kendrea Mekkah Griffith as Alice Coltrane, Duke Energy Theater at Spirit Square, Charlotte NC June 2013 | photo by Lovo

pg. 70 - (top pic) left to right: Stephen Gordon –drums, Kendrea Mekkah Griffith as Alice Coltrane, East to Edinburgh Festival, E 59 Theater, NYC 2009| photo by Lovo

pg. 70 - (bottom pic) left to right: John Colliani –piano, Stephen Gordon – drums, Kendrea Mekkah Griffith as Alice Coltrane, East to Edinburgh Festival, E 59 Theater, NYC 2009| photo by Lovo

pg. 71 - Quentin Talley as John Coltrane, Duke Energy Theater at Spirit Square, Charlotte NC June 2013 | photo by Lovo

Miles & Coltrane: Blue (.)

pg. 72 - left to right: Sultan Omar El-Amin as Miles Davis, Quentin Talley as John Coltrane, Duke Energy Theater at Spirit Square, Charlotte NC June 2013 | photo by Lovo

pg. 73 - Quentin Talley as John Coltrane, Duke Energy Theater at Spirit Square, Charlotte NC June 2013 | photo by Lovo

pg. 74 - Sultan Omar El-Amin as Miles Davis, Duke Energy Theater at Spirit Square, Charlotte NC June 2013 | photo by Lovo

pg. 76- Quentin Talley as John Coltrane, East to Edinburgh Festival, E 59 Theater, NYC 2009| photo by Lovo

pg. 77 - Sultan Omar El-Amin as Miles Davis, Quentin Talley as John Coltrane, Duke Energy Theater at Spirit Square, Charlotte NC June 2013 | photo by Lovo

pg. 80 - Sultan Omar El-Amin as Miles Davis, Quentin Talley as John Coltrane, Duke Energy Theater at Spirit Square, Charlotte NC June 2013 | photo by Lovo

pg. 82 - left to right: Tim Scott Jr. – drums, Charles Perry Jr. as The Storyteller, Tim Singh –Bass,, Duke Energy Theater at Spirit Square, Charlotte NC June 2013 | photo by Lovo

pg. 85 - (top pic) left to right: Sultan Omar El-Amin as Miles Davis, Miesha Ocean Rice as The Voice of The Pretty Face Strumpets, Ron Brendle –bass, Randolph Ward as Miles Davis (the here and now), Booth Playhouse, Charlotte, NC Nov 2008 | photo by Lovo

pg. 85 - (bottom pic) left to right: Sultan Omar El-Amin as Miles Davis (the human), Randolph Ward as Miles Davis (the here and now), East to Edinburgh Festival, E 59 Theater, NYC 2009| photo by Lovo

pg. 88 - left to right: Filmore Johnson as The Griot , Charles Perry Jr. as The Storyteller, McGlohon Theater at Spirit Square, Charlotte, NC June 2009 | photo by Lovo

pg. 91 - Sultan Omar El-Amin as Miles Davis , Duke Energy Theater at Spirit Square, Charlotte NC June 2013 | photo by Lovo

pg. 92 - Sultan Omar El-Amin as Miles Davis , Duke Energy Theater at Spirit Square, Charlotte NC June 2013 | photo by Lovo

pg. 93 - Quentin Talley as John Coltrane, Duke Energy Theater at Spirit Square, Charlotte NC June 2013 | photo by Lovo

pg. 98 – Marcus Jones –Saxophone, Duke Energy Theater at Spirit Square, Charlotte NC June 2013 | photo by Lovo

pg. 100 – left to right: Charles Perry Jr. as The Storyteller, Filmore Johnson as The Griot,, Duke Energy Theater at Spirit Square, Charlotte NC June 2013 | photo by Lovo

pg. 103 - Filmore Johnson as The Griot,, Duke Energy Theater at Spirit Square, Charlotte NC June 2013 | photo by Lovo

pg. 107 - left to right: Quentin Talley as John Coltrane, Sultan Omar El-Amin as Miles Davis, Outside The Jazz Bar, Edinburgh, Scotland, 2009 | photo by CP Maze

pg. 111 - Quentin Talley as John Coltrane, McGlohon Theater at Spirit Square, Charlotte NC June 2009| photo by Lovo

pg. 112- Sultan Omar El-Amin as Miles Davis, Booth Playhouse, Charlotte NC Nov 2008| photo by Lovo

pg. 115- Sultan Omar El-Amin as Miles Davis, Lynn Grissett Jr. –Trumpet, East to Edinburgh Festival, E 59 Theater, NYC 2009 | photo by Lovo

pg. 116 – Tim Scott Jr. –Drums, Duke Energy Theater at Spirit Square, Charlotte NC June 2013 | photo by Lovo

pg. 119 - Sultan Omar El-Amin as Miles Davis, McGlohon Theater at Spirit Square, Charlotte NC June 2009| photo by Lovo

pg. 120 – Kendrea Mekkah Griffith as Alice Coltrane, Duke Energy Theater at Spirit Square, Charlotte NC June 2013 | photo by Lovo

pg. 123 - left to right: Randolph Ward as Miles Davis (the here and now), Jhe Russell as John Coltrane (always trying to elevate), McGlohon Theater at Spirit Square, Charlotte NC June 2009| photo by Lovo

pg. 124 - Black Swan, Duke Energy Theater at Spirit Square, Charlotte NC June 2013 | photo by Lovo

pg. 129 – Eleazar Shafer –trumpet, Tim Scott Jr. –drums, Duke Energy Theater at Spirit Square, Charlotte NC June 2013 | photo by Lovo

pg. 130 - Randolph Ward as Miles Davis (the here and now), East to Edinburgh Festival, E 59 Theater, NYC 2009 | photo by Lovo

pg. 133 – Quentin Talley as John Coltrane, Duke Energy Theater at Spirit Square, Charlotte NC June 2013 | photo by Lovo

pg. 134 - left to right: Sultan Omar El-Amin as Miles Davis, Quentin Talley as John Coltrane, McGlohon Theater at Spirit Square, Charlotte NC June 2009| photo by Lovo

pg. 140 - Carlos Robson as Heroin, Duke Energy Theater at Spirit Square, Charlotte NC June 2013 | photo by Lovo

pg. 141 Sultan Omar El-Amin as Miles Davis, Duke Energy Theater at Spirit Square, Charlotte NC June 2013 | photo by Lovo

pg. 144 - Quentin Talley as John Coltrane, Stephen Gordon –drums, East to Edinburgh Festival, E 59 Theater, NYC 2009| photo by Lovo

pg. 145 - Quentin Talley as John Coltrane, Stephen Gordon –drums, East to Edinburgh Festival, E 59 Theater, NYC 2009| photo by Lovo

pg. 151- 2009-2011 poster, McGlohon Theater at Spirit Square, Charlotte NC June 2013 | photo by Lovo

Concrete Generation

www.ingramcontent.com/pod-product-compliance
Lightning Source LLC
Chambersburg PA
CBHW041621220426
43662CB00001B/6